UNTAMED
WONDERS

Amazing Facts About Wild Animals

(PART 1)

SHIVANI BHARDWAJ

WHY IS THIS BOOK FOR YOU?

"Untamed Wonders" is a captivating children's book that takes young readers on an exciting and educational journey into the enchanting world of wildlife.

Through colorful illustrations and engaging facts, this book is tailored to inspire a love for nature and a curiosity about the diverse creatures that share our planet. What makes "Untamed Wonders" perfect for children is its ability to balance fun and learning. The book introduces young readers to the wonders of the animal kingdom, fostering an early appreciation for the beauty and importance of nature.

Additionally, this book incorporates educational elements, teaching children about different species, habitats, lifespans, and the importance of the untamed spirit of wildlife. If you are looking for a children's book that combines the magic of amazing facts with educational value, "Untamed Wonders" is a perfect choice. It Promises to transport young readers into a world where imagination meets learning, making it an ideal addition to any child's library.

GLOSSARY

1. **Captivity:** It is the condition of being trapped. Animals that are kept in zoos are in captivity.

2. **Camouflage:** The way in which an animal's colour or shape matches its surroundings and makes it difficult to be spotted.

3. **Carnivores:** Any animal that eats meat.

4. **DNA:** Deoxyribonucleic acid(DNA) is a molecule that carries genetic information for the development and functioning of an organism.

5. **Endangered:** Animals that are in danger of disappearing from the world.

6. **Grassland:** A large area of open land covered with wild grass.

7. **Guzzle:** To eat or drink too fast and too much.

8. **Herbivores:** An animal that only eats grass and plants.

9. **Mammal:** An animal of the type that gives birth to live babies, not eggs and feeds its young on milk from its own body.

10. **Nocturnal:** Awake and active at night and asleep during the day.

11.   **Omnivore:** An animal that eats both plants and meat.

12.   **Predators:** An animal that kills and eats other animals.

13.   **Prey:** An animal that is killed and eaten by another animal.

14.   **Savannah:** A wide flat open area of land, especially in Africa, that is covered with grass but has few trees.

15.   **Scavenger:** An animal that feeds on the remains of other animals or eats decomposing plant or animal matter.

16.   **Woodland:** land that has a lot of trees growing on it.

TABLE OF CONTENTS

CHAPTER #01: LION

SPECIFICATION

Scientific name: Panthera Leo

Class: Mammalia

Order: Carnivore

Food in nature: Buffalo, Zebra, Giraffe, Antelop etc.

Habitat: They like to live in open woodland, thick grassland, and brush habitat.

Life span: 15 years in the wild and 30 years in captivity.

AMAZING FACTS ABOUT LION

1. Nearly all wild lions live in Africa, but one small population exist elsewhere.

2. Male lions can weigh up to 30 stones.

3. They start off spotty.

4. They hunt during storms.

5. Lions are big eaters.

6. Lions are symbols of strength and courage. They are also common symbols for royalty and stateliness.

7. Their coats are yellow-gold and that range in color from blond to reddish brown to black.

8. Lions are the only cats that live in groups.

9. A group, or pride can be up to 30 lions, depending on how much food and water is available.

10. Female lions are the main hunters.

11. A lion's roar can be heard up to 8 Km away.

12. Lions scent mark their territory using their wee, to create a border.

13. Lions are Primarily Nocturnal (active at night).

14. The scientific name for lions is Panthera Leo.

15. A lion's heels don't touch the ground when it walks.

16. A female lion needs 5 kg of meat a day. A male needs 7 kg or more a day.

17. Simba, weighing 380 kg is the heaviest lion on record till date. He was kept captive at Colchester zoo in England.

18. Lions are social.

19. Lions don't need to drink everyday but they do need to eat.

20. African lions are the most social of all big cats and live together in groups or prides. A pride consists of about 15 lions.

21. You can gauge the age of a male lion by looking at its mane.

22. Lions can change direction quickly when chasing prey.

23. When a lion is angry or feeling threatened it will sweep its tail from side to side.

24. If it is hunting it will keep its tail stiff & twitch it from time to time.

25. Lions roar a bit like babies cry.

26. Lions love to take bath in rain and seemingly enjoying it.

27. Lions can go up to four days without drinking water.

28. Lioness will keep her cubs hidden from large birds, snake and even male lions for around six weeks until they are old enough to follow the pride.

29. Lions can climbs trees (if they have to).

30. **Question:** How do lions hunt? Which kind of hunting tactics they use.
    Answer: Lions strategy is different according to the size and strength of the prey. Lions use a co- operative

strategy for big animals. While attacking on zebra, cape, buffalo or wild beest , they first encircle or cover the herd from all the sides. After they get closer they charge upon the group.

CHAPTER #02: TIGER

SPECIFICATION

Scientific name: Panthera tigris

Class: Mammalia

Order: Carnivora

Food in nature: They eat variety of prey ranging in size from termites to elephants calves, wild boar, deer, buffalo, sloth etc.

Habitats: Rainforests, grasslands, savannas and even mangrove swamps.

Life span: In wild 11 years and in captivity 20 to 25 years.

AMAZING FACTS ABOUT TIGER

1. Tiger stripes are unique.

2. Tigers can use their ears to communicate.

3. Like the human fingerprint each tiger's stripe patteren is one of a kind. Individual tigers are identified by their unique stripes.

4. A tigress uses the white spots on the back of her ears to communicate with her cubs. They act as a flasher to the cubs. When a tigress senses danger she flattens her

ears and the cub's respond by crouching down and hiding.

5.   One meal a week. Tiger primarily hunt deer but as opportunistic predators, they can also eat wild bear,birds,fish,rodents, amphibians reptiles and even insects.

6.   For tigers only one in ten hunts are successful a large deer can provide a tiger with one week's food.

7.   Tigers are Endangered. (Explanation : this means they are considered to be facing a very high risk of extinction in the wild).

8.   They are protective over their kill. (Explanation : tiger don't usually eat their prey at the kill site but instead drag their prey into cover to feed . if a tiger leaves say to get a drink it will cover its kill by raking leaves, dirt, grass and even rocks over the carcass).

9.   A punch from a tiger may kill you.

10.   Tigers are nocturnal animals.

11.   Tigers cubs are born blind and only half of cubs survive.

12.   Tigers love to swim and play in the water. (Explanation :they even have the ability to kill the prey in the water and as adult, it is said that they can swim

for several kilometers and even reported one to swim for 30 km in just a day).

13.   Tigers live for about 25 years.

14.   A group of tigers are called ambush or streak.

15.   Tiger have antiseptic saliva. Usually they do is, they tend to lick the area in order to prevent any infection.

16.   It is also said that tigers are less likely to attack when we see them in fact most of the villagers in India wear a face mask on the back of their head just to trick the tigers. (Explanation: this is because ,if you look a tiger in its eyes it is less likely to kill you.)

17.   Tigers live alone and move chiefly at night.

CHAPTER #03: GIRAFFES

SPECIFICATION

Scientific name: Giraffa Camelopardalis

Class: Mammle

Order: Artiodactyls

Food in nature: Leaves and buds on trees and shrubs, herbs, climbers, vines and preferred flower and fruit.

Habitat: Semi-arid savannah and savannah woodlands in Africa.

Life span: In wild 25 years and in captivity up to 27 years.

AMAZING FACTS ABOUT GIRAFFES

1. Giraffes are the tallest mammals on the earth. Their legs alone are taller than many humans about 6 feet.

2. They can run as fast as 35 miles an hour over short distances, or cruise at 10 mph over longer distances.

3. Giraffes only need to drink once evenly few days. Most of their water comes from all the plants they eat.

4. Giraffes spend most of their lives standing up, they even sleep and give birth standing up.

5.   A giraffe's spot are much like human finger prints. No two individual giraffes have exactly the same pattern.

6.   Giraffes have hair covered horns called ossicones.

7.   Giraffes are super peaceful animals.

8.   Giraffes new born are taller than most humans.

9.   Giraffes live primarily in Savanna areas in the Sub-Saharan region of Africa.

10.   Step taken by the Giraffe are about 15 feet in length.

11.   The kick of Giraffes is so strong that it can also kill a lion.

12.   Giraffes flick insects away with their tongue.

13.   Giraffes tongues are dark bluish in color.

14.   Giraffes are herbivores they only eat plants.

15.   A female giraffe is called a cow and male giraffe is called a bull.

16.   No one has ever seen a giraffe swimming.

17.   A group of giraffes are called towers.

18.   A giraffe can clean their ears with their tongue.

19.   There is a hotel in Kenya, where you can hang out with Giraffes all days.

20. There are four species of Giraffes :Northern Giraffe, Southern Giraffe, Masai Giraffe and reticulated Giraffe.

21. Giraffes are the National animal of Tanzania.

22. Giraffe is sometime known as stink bulls.

CHAPTER #04: ZEBRA

SPECIFICATION

Scientific name: Genus Equus.

Class: Mammal

Order: Perissodactyla

Food in nature: Mostly graze, or nibble on grass, but will also eat stems, leaves and bark when grass is not available.

Habitat: Savannahs, grasslands, woodlands, shrub lands and mountainous areas.

Life span: Average life span 15- 18 years in wild and 25-30 years in captivity.

AMAZING FACTS ABOUT ZEBRA

1. Zebra are native to Africa and closely related to horses.

2. Zebras have three subspecies the:

    1. Grevy's Zebra

    2. Plains Zebra

    3. Mountain Zebra

3. Zebra stripes are unique like human fingerprints. (No two Zebras alike have the same stripes)

4.	**Question:** Why Zebra has stripes ?

Ans: The basic idea is that the black stripes absorb heat from the sun and warm up Zebras during the early morning, while the white stripes reflect more light and help them cool off while they stand and graze in the blazing sun of Africa all day.

5.	Zebra can sleep standing up during day.

6.	Zebra can communicate non-verbaly with their ears.

7.	All Zebras live in Africa.

8.	Zebra are herbivores. They generally eat grass, leaves, twigs and sometimes bark from trees.

9.	Zebra can run fast between 40-43 mph.

10.	Zebra considred as endangered species.

11.	The Grevy's Zebra was given its name in honor of a past monarch.

12.	Mountain Zebra are impressive climbers.

13.	Plain Zebras sense a predator they use a high pitched sound to alert the herd.

14.	Mountain Zebra do not have stripes on their bellies.

15.	They have several forms of self defense.

16.	Each species has different types of stripes.

17.   Zebra serve as a famous mascot.

18.   **Question:** Are zebras white with black stripes or black with white stripes?

      Answer: Zebras are like nature's amazing artwork. Their fur is black and those cool stripes you see are actually white. Because if you shave a zebra it would be almost completely black. So that zebras are black with white stripes.

19.   A Zebra will shake its entire body to release stress.

20.   Zebra spend around 60- 80 % of their time eating.

21.   Zebra have a good sense of smell, taste and hearing.

22.   Zebra teeth never stop growing because of constant grazing wears them down.

23.   Zebra can survive up to 5 days without water.

24.   There are golden Zebras do exist. They have abnormal pigmentation that makes them have white skin with golden stripes.

25.   Zoo Zebras live longer than wild Zebras.

CHAPTER #05: ELEPHANT

SPECIFICATION

Scientific name: Loxodonta

Class: Mammilla

Order: Proboscidea

Food in nature: grasses, leaves, shrubs, fruits and roots.

Habitat: Wetlands, forest, grassland, savanna and desert across 37 countries in southern, eastern, western and central Africa.

Life span: Asian elephant - 48 years, African bush elephant and African forest elephant- 60-70 years.

AMAZING FACTS ABOUT ELEPHANT

1. Elephants are the largest living land animals. There are three living species that are currently recognized.

    1. The African bust elephant

    2. The African forest elephant

    3. The Asian elephant

2. Like humans, elephants have teeth called incisors.

3. Elephants have a total of 26 teeth including their two incisors (tusk).

4. Elephants lose their molar not once in their lives- but six times.

5. African elephants have larger ears and Asian elephants have smaller ears.

6. Elephants have around 15,000 muscle units in their trunk.

7. Elephants can also communicate through seismic signals sounds that create vibration in the ground which may they detect through their bone.

8. An elephant never forgets.

9. Elephants are herbivores. They have a big appetite.

10. Elephants are excellent swimmers.

11. Elephant use mud as sunscreen. Elephants get sunburned because of their sensitive skin. They love to play in dirt and they often throw mud or clay on themselves as a layer of protection.

12. Asian elephants have math skill.

13. The elephant trunk serve as a nose, a hand, an extra foot, a signalling device and tool for gathering food, siphoning water, dusting, digging etc.

14.   Elephants can recognize themselves in a mirror.

15.   Elephants sense of smell is very strong. They can use their sense of smell to detect predators, locate water sources and establish which elephant is part of their family.

16.   In wild they can choose safe plants for food by smelling.

17.   Elephant can live for up to seventy years.

18.   An elephant poop is great for environment.

19.   African Elephants have two "fingers" at the end of their trunks, where as Asian elephants have one.

20.   Both male and female African elephants grow tusk, but only male Asian elephant grow them. Female Asian elephants don't have tusks.

21.   An adult male elephant can drink up to 212 L of water in less than 5 minutes.

22.   Asian elephant have more hair on their body then African elephants.

23.   Elephants have a slow pulse rate of twentyseven.

24.   Elephants can urinate approximate 50 liters throughout the day.

25. Female elephants are called "cows" and male elephants are called "Bulls" and babies are called "calves".

26. Elephants are the only mammals that cannot jump.

27. Baby elephant are born blind.

28. After humans elephants are the only animals to have chins.

29. Elephants sometimes suck their trunks when they feel nervous.

CHAPTER #06: HIPPOPOTAMUS

SPECIFICATION

Scientific name: Hippopotamus Amphibious

Class: Mammalia

Order: Artiodactyla

Food in nature: Short grasses, fruits

Habitat: Lives along the rivers and lakes throughout sub-Saharan Africa.

Life span: In wild 40-50 years and in captivity 61 years.

AMAZING FACTS ABOUT HIPPOPOTAMUS

1. Hippos are large semi-aquatic mammals with a large barrel shaped body, short legs, short tail and an enormous head.

2. Hippopotamus can hold their breath under water for about 5 minutes.

3. To stay cool in the blistering African heat, hippos spend most of their day in rivers and lakes.

4. Hippo sweats an oily red liquid from skin which helps to protect their skin from drying out and acts as a sun block too.

5. Hippos are herbivores and eat mostly grass. They can guzzle down up to 35 kg of their favorite grub in just one night.

6. Most Hippos are active at night.

7. Hippos usually live in groups or herds and lead by one large dominant male and other members are females and their young ones.

8. Female hippos called cows and give birth every two years.

9. Hippos eyes, nose and ears are located on the top of their head , which means they can see and breathe whistle submerged in the water.

10. Hippos can grows up to 15 feet long and weigh up to 8000 pounds.

11. Hippopotamus also known as "River horse" due to its bulky shape and tendency to spend time submerged in rivers and lakes.

12. Hippos are regarded as one of the most dangerous animals in the Africa.

13. There are two types of species of hippopotamus.

   1. The pigmy hippopotamus

   2. Common Hippopotamus

14.   Hippos can identify a friend or enemies by smelling their dung or poops.

15.   Hippos are found in many African countries with a suitable wetland habitat.

16.   Hippos have 36 teeth that include one canine, two incisors, three premolars one on each side of their jaws.

17.   Some hippos may have up to 40 teeth.

18.   Hippo canine teeth continue to grow and can even reach up to 50 cm in length.

19.   A hippopotamus can open its jaws really wide up to 150 degrees.

20.   In wild hippos live for around 40 years and in captivity they tend to live longer and may reach up to 50 years old.

CHAPTER #07: GORILLA

SPECIFICATION

Scientific name: Gorilla beringei, gorilla gorilla

Class: Mammilia

Order: Primates

Food in nature: Eat roots, shoots, fruit, wild celery, and tree bark and pulp.

Habitat: Lowland tropical rainforests of central Africa, montane rainforest and in bamboo forest.

Life span: 35-40 years in wild and 50 and more in captivity.

AMAZING FACTS ABOUT GORILLAS

1. Gorillas, the largest living Primates make their homes in central and east Africa.

2. There are two species of Gorillas

    a) Eastern Gorillas

    b) Western Gorillas

3. All wild gorillas live in central Africa.

4.   Gorillas are very social animals that live together in groups and their group known as troops.

5.   Adult males are known as 'Silverbacks' for the white hair that develops on age. These powerful males can be more than 10 times stronger than an average human.

6.   They can tear down banana trees, bend iron bars and bite with more power than a lion.

7.   Gorillas are very clever. Wild Gorillas use sticks to work out the depth of rivers and streams making ladders from bamboo to help baby Gorillas to reach the treetops.

8.   Gorilla nose prints are as unique as human fingerprints.

9.   A captive gorilla called 'koko' learned sign language and English words.

10.   Hanabi-ko, known as 'koko' was a female westerned low land gorilla. She learned 1000 signs and was able to understand more than 2000 English words over her lifetime.

11.   Koko created many beautiful paintings throughout her life.

12. Gorillas are herbivores animals. They stick to mainly vegetarian diet feeding on stems bamboo shoots and fruits.

13. Gorillas share 98.3% of their DNA with humans. They are our closet cousins after chimpanzee and Bonbons.

14. Their arms are longer than their legs.

15. Mountain gorillas are most fascinating animals. They are a subspecies of the eastern gorilla. The other subspecies being the eastern lowland gorilla.

16. Mountain gorillas cannot survive in a captive environment of the zoo.

17. This means that all those other Gorillas in wildlife zoos are not mountain gorillas.

18. They walk on the knuckles of their hands which is called knuckle walking.

19. Gorillas create nests on both the ground as well as trees to sleep in. They build their sleeping nest everyday with either tree branches or leaves where they sleep and move on the next day.

20. Mountain Gorillas are not complete vegetarians though they also eat ants and insects on occasion.

21.   Gorillas can catch human diseases. This is why coughing or sneezing is prohibited during a gorilla's trekking trip.

Note: If you have any communicable Disease, you will not be allowed to go into the forest to see gorillas.

22.   Gorillas are gentle giants and display many human like behaviors and emotions such as laughter and sadness.

23.   Infant gorillas are smaller than human infants when they are born.

24.   The eastern lowland gorillas also known as Grauer's gorilla and is the largest of the four gorilla subspecies.

25.   Gorillas very rarely need to drink water, because they consume succulent (juicy) vegetation that is comprised of almost half water as well as morning dew.

CHAPTER #08: RHINO

SPECIFICATION

Scientific name: Rhinocerotidae

Class: Mammalia

Order: Perissodactyla

Food in nature: Grass and the fruit and leaves of shrubs and trees.

Habitat: Tropical and subtropical grassland, savannas and shrub lands, tropical moist forests, deserts and shrub lands.

Life span: Vary on species. White rhinoceros 40-50 years, Indian rhinoceros 35-45 years, black rhinoceros 35-50 years.

AMAZING FACTS ABOUT RHINO

1. There are 5 species of Rihno in the world.

2. Rhino can weigh over 3 tonnes (3000kg).

3. Rhinos are herbivores (Plant eaters) and have to eat a lot each day to be full.

4. The name rhinoceros means' nose horn'.

5. White Rhinos are the 2nd largest land mammal in the world.

6. A group of rhinos is known as a herd or a crash.

7. Rhinos can run at 30-40 miles per hour.

8. Rhinos communicate by doing a poop.

9. Greater one-horned Rhinos can swim and even dive underwater.

10. Earth is home to five species of Rhinoceros- the black rhino and the white rhino which live in Africa and the Sumatran, Javan and Indian (Greater one horned) rhino, which inhabit the tropical forests and swamps of Asia.

11. These brilliant beasts are known for their awesome, giant horns that grow from their snouts.

12. Javan and Indian rhinos have one horn, where as the white, black and Sumatran rhinos have two horns.

13. They love to get mucky in fact mud protects their skin from the strong sun and wards off biting bugs too.

14. Each individual's rhino dung smell unique.

15. Rhinos have poor vision. They are unable to motionless person at a distance of 30 m. they mainly rely on their strong sense of smell.

16. The oxpeckers(a bird) lives on rhino and eats all of the bugs and parasites on the animal. Rhino benefits from having bugs removed.

17. When there is a danger to the rhino the oxpecker flies high and makes much noise in order to alert nearby animals to the danger.

18. Rhinos come in variety of shapes and size.

19. Average height of a rhino is around 1.8 m.

20. The heaviest rhino is the Indian/ greater –one-horned rhino.

21. White rhinos usually have the longest horns.

22. Some Javan rhino females have no horn at all.

23. The horn of a rhino does not have a bone and it is not attached to the rhino's skull. It is made up of keratin.

24. Rhino horns are solid and not hollow and continue to grow throughout the rhino's lifetime.

25. If a rhino survives a poacher's attack on its horn a new one will grow back.

26. The chubbiest rhino is also called a unicorn and is built like a knight in the shining armor.

27. The nickname of the greater one horned or Indian rhino is the unicorn rhino.

28. White rhinos have flat wide and broad mouth with square lips. They are called "grazers" since they eat grass from the ground.

29. Black rhinos are called "browsers" because they have beak shaped lips that they use to grasp leaves and twigs from trees when they eating.

30. A white rhino's head can weigh over 200lbs (970kg).

31. Rhinos can't see anything until its almost right in front of them.

32. Rhinos can't jump.

33. Rhinos are the only animals that are not afraid of fire.

34. Rhinos identify one another by their smell.

35. Each rhino smell is unique.

CHAPTER #09: KANGAROOS

SPECIFICATION

Scientific name: Macropus

Class: Mammalia

Order: Diprotodontia

Food in nature: As herbivores that eat grasses, as well as leaves, ferns, flowers, fruit and moss.

Habitat: Number of habitats in Tasmania, Australia, and nearby islands, such as trees, plains, woodlands, and savannas.

Life span: 8 years in wild and 25 years in captivity.

AMAZING FACTS ABOUT KANGAROOS

1. Kangaroos possess powerful hind leg, a long strong tail and small front legs.

2. Kangaroos belong to the animal family Macropus literally 'big foot'.

3. Female kangaroos sport a pouch on their belly to cradle baby kangaroos called joeys.

4. Newborn joeys are just one inch long at birth.

5. Kangaroos live in eastern Australia.

6.   They live in small groups called troops or herd or mobs.

7.   There are 60 species of kangaroo and one of them climbs trees. They can hop 8 meters (25 feet) in a single bound.

8.   Their tail is used as a fifth limb (arm).

9.   They can't move backward because of their long feet and large tail. Kangaroos can't walk or hop backwards.

10.   Kangaroo appears on the Australian coat of arms, representing a nation that is always moving forward.

11.   Female kangaroos can pause their pregnancies and give birth when conditions are right.

12.   They have plenty of ways to communicate with each other including nose touching, stomping their hind legs and growling.

13.   Red kangaroos are the largest species of kangaroo.

14.   Kangaroos are herbivores and like to chew on grasses, herbs and shrubs.

15.   Kangaroos need very little water to survive and are capable of going for months without drinking at all.

16. Male kangaroos are called bucks, boomers or jacks. Females are flyers or jills. Baby kangaroos are called joeys.

17. Kangaroos are powerful kickers. They sometimes wrestle too. Their kick is painful and damaging.

18. Male kangaroos have thickened skin around their bellies to protect themselves from these powerful kicks.

19. They have excellent hearing power & keen eyesight.

20. The kangaroo does not have a very long lifespan in the wild. Its average lifespan is only about 5 years but it can live up to 25 years in captivity such as in a zoo or animal sanctuary.

CHAPTER #10: BEAR

SPECIFICATION

Scientific name: Ursidae

Class: Mammalia

Order: Carnivora

Food in nature: Bear is omnivorous and eat berries, grain, fish, insects, birds and mammals.

Habitat: America, Europe, and Asia

Life span: 25 years in the wild and 50 years in captivity.

AMAZING FACTS ABOUT BEAR

1. Bear are extraordinarily intelligent animals. They have far superior navigation skills to humans, excellent memories.

2. Bear have excellent senses of smell, sight and hearing. They can smell food, cubs, and a predators from miles away. Their great eyesight allows them to detect when fruits are ripe.

3. Some species of Asiatic bear build nests in the trees. They can use these for hiding, eating and even sleeping.

4.   The bear is a common national personification for Russia and Germany. The brown bear is Finland's national animal.

5.   There are 8 bear species in the world.

6.   There are several species of bear. They are the polar bear, the brown bear, the black bear, the Asiatic black bear, the sun bear, the spectacled bear and the sloth bear.

7.   The brown bear is commonly called the grizzly bear.

8.   The most common way for a bear to mark its territory is by rubbing against trees and other plants, bears may also bite and claw away the bark of a tree mark territory.

9.   At birth, bear cubs are blind and they can weight only around 400g.

10.   Some species of Asiatic bear build nests in the trees.

11.   The sun bear is smallest of all the bear. It gets name from a blond chest patch of fur that looks like a setting sun. Sun bear are also known as honey bears.

12.   Canada is known as the polar bear capital of the world.

13.   Bears have two layers of fur, a short layer of fur keeps the bear warm and the long layer keeps water away from the skin and short fur.

14.   Polar bears on a average can swim nonstop for over 60 miles.

15.   Polar bears love the cold which is why the Arctic Circle is the perfect home.

16.   Polar bears can be as tall as 10 feet, and they are amazing swimmers.

17.   Polar bears are the largest land carnivores in the world.

18.   All bears except polar bears and giant pandas are omnivores.

19.   Bears have unique nose prints.

20.   Sloth bear activity hunts insects using sticky tongues. Their diet includes ants, termites, wasps and bees.

21.   Bears make their dens using their claws to burrow out enough space for themselves.

22.   Bears don't have whiskers. They do have hairs that grow on their snout, but these do not have the sensory capability.

23.   Bears aren't social animals.

CHAPTER #11: HYENA

SPECIFICATION

Scientific name: Hyaenidae

Class: Mammalia

Order: Carnivora

Food in nature: They are carnivores who eat other mammals like zebra, grazelles, giraffes, birds, rabbits, snakes, insects, wild dog etc.

Habitat: They live in habitats such as semi- deserts, savannas and open woodland, and dense dry woodland.

Life span: 12 years in wild, and 23 years in captivity.

AMAZING FACTS ABOUT HYENA

1. Hyenas are perhaps most famous for their uncanny laughter and their tendency to scavenger leftover from large predators.

2. These fierce animals roam great distance at night to find food.

3. There are four living species of hyena. They include the spotted hyena striped hyena, the brown hyena and the aardwolf.

4.   The four hyena species differ by size, behaviors, appearance.

5.   Hyenas can be classified into two main types:

   (1) Dog like hyenas

   (2) Bone crushing hyenas.

6.   Female hyenas are more dominant in their social circles than male.

7.   Each spotted hyena has a signature "whoop" which other clan members can recognize and their calls can indicate their rank and age.

8.   As scavengers, hyenas evolved the ability to not just crush and swallow bones but to fully digest them.

9.   Hyena dens often have bare patches or leftover bones near the entrance.

10.   Hyenas have good night vision and hearing, making it easier for them to hunt at night or listen for predators.

11.   These amazing animals inhabit savannahs, grasslands, woodlands and forest edges across sub-Saharan Africa.

12.   They live in territorial social group called clans. Clans are dominated by females and can reach up to 70 members.

13. Hyenas are capable of digesting bones horns and even the teeth of their prey.

14. Spotted hyenas are the largest hyena species.

15. Brown hyena has the shortest life span of all hyena species.

16. The hyena is more closely related to the mongoose and cat than the dog.

17. Female hyenas possess similar looking reproductive organs to male.

18. The hyena is primarily a hunter, not a scavenger. They usually hunt alone however clans will hunt together in order to catch larger prey. They are also good opportunistic hunters.

19. Hyenas also tend to dig up and scavenge on human corpses (dead body).

20. All hyena species make dens where they sleep, give birth and nurse their young ones.

21. Hyenas have their powerful jaws and possess the strongest bite force among mammals.

22. Exceptional night vision gives hyenas an advantage during their nocturnal activities such as hunting and scavenging.

23.   Hyenas are skilled hunters.

CHAPTER #12: CHIMPANZEE

SPECIFICATION

Scientific name: Pan troglodytes

Class: Mammalia

Order: Primates

Food in nature: They are omnivorous frugivores and eat fruits, roots, nuts, leaves, plants, flowers, insects, meat and more.

Habitat: Savanna, woodlands, grassland- forest mosaics and tropical moist forests.

Life span: 31 years for male and 38 years for female in wild and 66 years and more in captivity.

AMAZING FACTS ABOUT CHIMPANZEES

1. The chimpanzees also known as simply the chimp. Chimpanzee is a species of great ape.

2. Chimpanzees are found across central and west Africa.

3. Chimpanzees are our closet living relatives, sharing 98.7% of our genetic blueprint.

4. Chimpanzees are omnivores. That means they eat all sorts of vegetarian food as well as animals.

5.   Baby chimps will have a white tail tuft.

6.   Chimpanzees can't swim.

7.   They are known to play intentive games when they are bored.

8.   Chimpanzee can make over 30 different noises and the most common noise their species make is known as the long pant-hoot.

9.   Long pant hoot noise is used as a long- distance call for a variety of social reasons.

10.   They have the ability to learn human languages such as sign language.

11.   Chimpanzees can live up to 80 years.

12.   Chimps can walk on two legs.

13.   Chimpanzee's intelligence varies just as human's intelligence. Some chimpanzees are brilliant and some are less intelligent.

14.   Adult chimpanzees have 32 teeth.

15.   There are three species of chimpanzees, which live in different areas. Chimpanzee is covered almost all over its body with long, back hairs. The hairs become grayer as the animal ages.

16. They have long arms that extended below their knees, short legs and black hair covering almost their entire body. Their faces are flat with big eyes, a small nose and a wide mouth.

CHAPTER #13- LEOPARD

SPECIFICATION

Scientific name: Panthera pardus

Class: Mammalia

Order: carnivora

Food in nature: Baboons, hares, rodents, birds, lizards, porcupines, warthogs, fish and dung beetles.

Habitat: Forests, subtropical & tropical regions, savannas, grasslands, deserts, and rocky and mountain regions.

Life span: 12-15 years in wild and 23 years in captivity.

AMAZING FACTS ABOUT LEOPARD

1. Leopard is one of the five extant species in the genus Panthera.

2. It has a pale yellowish to dark golden fur with dark spots grouped in rosettes.

3. Leopard spots are called rosettes.

4. Leopards like to spend time in trees.

5. Leopards are smallest of the big cats.

6. Leopards are fast runners.

7.   Leopards are solitary animals.

8.   Leopards are Ambush predators.

9.   Leopards cubs are born blind and helpless and rely on their mother for protection.

10.   Leopards are strong swimmers and are able to catch fish and aquatic prey.

11.   They are able to run at speeds of up to 58 km (36 miles) per hour.

12.   They are able to survive in a variety of different habitats including grasslands, forests, deserts and mountains.

13.   Leopards have unique hunting technique where they will drag their prey into trees to keep it safe from other predators.

14.   Leopards are able to kill their prey with a powerful bite to the neck.

15.   Leopard are known as "ghosts of the forest".

16.   Female leopards are known for their mothering skills and will fiercely protect their cubs from predators.

17.   The spots on a leopard's coat are unique to each individual, similar to human fingerprints.

18. Leopards are able to survive for long periods without water, obtaining moisture from the blood of their prey.

19. Leopards have binocular vision that is important for catching fast moving prey.

20. Leopard's tail is proportionally longer than that of the lion or tiger.

21. Leopard's forefeet larger than hind feet.

22. Largest subspecies of leopard is Persian leopard up to 90 kg and smallest subspecies is Arabian leopard 20-30 kg.

23. The purpose of leopard spots is to camouflage it is so that can move and hunt undetected.

24. The lion is probably the biggest enemy of the leopard and a fight to the death will ensure when they come into contact.

CHAPTER #14: ORANGUTANS

SPECIFICATION

Scientific Name: Pongo

Class: Mammalia

Order: Primates

Food in nature: Fruits, leaves, flowers, insects and even small mammals.

Habitat: Rainforests of southeast asian islands of borneo and Sumatra.

Life span: In wild 35-40 years and 50 in captivity.

AMAZING FACTS ABOUT ORANGUTANS

1.   There are 3 species of orangutan.

2.   Orangutans are the heaviest tree dwelling animals.

3.   They have got long arms.

4.   Orangutans are the world's largest tree climbing mammals.

5.   They are the largest arboreal mammals and the most socially solitary of the great apes.

6.   Orangutans live up to 60 years or more.

7.   Orangutans have incredibly close bonds with their mother.

8.   Orangutans are red haired apes that live in the tropical rainforests of Sumatra and Borneo in Southeast Asia.

9.   These magnificent mammals measure 1.2m to 1.5 m tall and weigh up to 100kg.

10.   Orangutan seriously big arm span some males can stretch their arms 2m from fingertip.

11.   They are day time eaters, their diet consist mostly of fruits and leaves but they also eat nuts, bark, insects and once in a while, bird eggs too.

12.   In Malay and Indonesian orang means "person" and utan is derived from hutan which means "forest" thus orangutan means "person of the forest."

13.   Orangutans eat 300 types of fruits.

14.   Their favorite fruit is the diurnal tree fruit this is one of the worse smelling fruits in the world and can be described as smelling like sewage water.

15.   Orangutans share the same DNA with human.

16.   They are our closet relatives after apes.

17.   Like other animals, orangutans make nests that they can sleep in. They do this in 10 minutes by pulling together branches.

18.   Some orangutans use tools. They use tools like sticks to get termites, ants or bees out of tree holes.

19.   Orangutans have also been observed making a 'glove' out of leaves when handling pricky fruits or throny branches.

20.   Some male orangutans develop large cheek pads on their face.

21.   Orangutan has opposable thumbs and toes.

22.   Orangutans are critically endangered.

23.   Females orangutans only give birth once every eight years which is longer than any other animals.

CHAPTER #15: BISON

SPECIFICATION

Scientific name: Bison

Class: Mammalia

Order: Artiodactyla

Food in nature: Herbaceous grasses and sedges.

Habitat: Grassland and open savannas of North America.

Life span: 15 years in wild and 25 years in captivity.

AMAZING FACTS ABOUT BISON

1. Bison are the largest mammal in North America. Male bison (called bulls) weigh up to 2,000 pounds and stand 6 feet tall.

2. You can judge a bison's mood by its tail. When it hangs down and switches naturally the bison is usually calm. If the tail is standing straight up. Watch out it may be ready to charge.

3. Bison can run faster than horse. They can run up to 35 miles per hour.

4. A baby bison has a nickname 'Red Dog'.

5. Bison eat different types of grasses and sedges. In winter months when grass is harder to find then they will also eat twigs and shrubs.

6. Both male and female bison have horns.

7. American bison is not related to the water buffalo or the African buffalo, American bison is more closely related to cows and goats.

8. Bison can plow snow with their heads.

9. Baby bison are an orange- red –color until they are few months old.

10. Bison are nearsighted or poor eyesight but they have great sense of hearing.

11. The American bison is the official mammal to the United States.

12. The group of Bison is called herd.

13. Bison can jump as 6 vertical feet as well as can spin around quickly.

14. There are two subspecies of bison in North America:

    1. The plain bison

    2. The wood bison

15. Bison's thick covering is highly effective in protecting them from cold and snow.

16. Bison have significantly more hair than cattle.

17. Bison play key roles in maintain the balance of the ecosystem.

18. Bison roll in the dirt for several reasons.

19. A wild bison's lifespan is about 25 years.

SUMMARY

"**Untamed Wonders**" is an Enthralling exploration into the captivating world of wildlife, bringing young readers face to face with the untamed beauty and diversity of the animal kingdom.

Young readers find himself/herself immersed in the intricate dance between predator and prey, survival and instinct, and the delicate balance of the ecosystem.

This book tells us which animal shares the DNA with humans ? Why does Zebra have strips?

Which animal's new born baby is taller than human?

How does a tigress communicate with her cubs?

Which kind of hunting tactics does lion use?

This book is a portal into the extraordinary lives of these creatures an exploration of their habitats, behaviours and the delicate balance that binds them to the earth.

ABOUT THE AUTHOR

Shivani Bhardwaj is an accomplished author and educator with a passion for science and education.

With a **Master's** degree in **Chemistry** and a **Bachelor's** degree in **Education,** she combines her academic expertise with her love for teaching.

For the past seven years, Shivani has been inspiring young minds as a dedicated teacher, *helping students unlock the wonders of the world through the lens of science.*

Beyond her professional pursuits, Shivani is a devoted homemaker who believes in the power of knowledge and exploration. Her curiosity about the natural world led her to embark on a remarkable journey of discovery. Drawing from her extensive research and personal experiences, Shivani has authored a captivating book entitled.

Check her earlier book at the below link:

https://www.azonlinks.com/bc/65ODA

MAY I ASK YOU A FAVOR?

At the outset, I want to give you a big thanks for reading this book. You could have chosen any other book, but you took mine, and I appreciate this. I hope you have at least a few actionable insights that will positively impact your daily life.

Can I ask for 30 seconds more of your time?

I'd love it if you could leave a review of the book. That will help me grow my readership by encouraging folks to take a chance on my books.

Keeping it straight - reviews are the lifeblood of any author.

It will take less than a minute of your time but will tremendously help me reach out to more people. Kindly provide your review at the store you bought this book from. And I'd love to see your review. Thanks for your support.

www.ingramcontent.com/pod-product-compliance
Lightning Source LLC
Chambersburg PA
CBHW050738260726

48661CB00001B/289